UNITED STATES
AIRBORNE FORCES
1940-1986

49070

BLANDFORD WAR
PHOTO-FILES

UNITED STATES
AIRBORNE FORCES
1940-1986
LEROY THOMPSON

BLANDFORD PRESS
POOLE · NEW YORK · SYDNEY

First published in the UK 1986 by Blandford Press
Link House, West Street, Poole, Dorset BH15 1LL

Copyright © 1986 Leroy Thompson

Distributed in the United States by
Sterling Publishing Co, Inc,
2 Park Avenue, New York, NY 10016

Distributed in Australia by
Capricorn Link (Australia) Pty Ltd
PO Box 665, Lane Cove, NSW 2066

ISBN 0 7137 1527 8 (hardback)
ISBN 0 7137 1544 8 (paperback)

Typeset by Poole Typesetting (Wessex) Ltd.
Printed in Great Britain by Bath Press, Bath

CONTENTS

I TRODUCTIO

The United States lagged behind the Soviet Union, Italy and Germany in starting to train parachute troops, though it should be noted that Billy Mitchell had suggested training the 1st Infantry Division in the parachute role during World War One. The first unit to be formed in the US Army specifically in the airborne role was the Parachute Test Platoon of 50 men which came into existence in July 1940. The Test Platoon evolved into the 1st Parachute Platoon and then into the 501st Parachute Battalion. By October 1941, four parachute battalions — 501st, 502nd, 503rd and 504th — were in existence. After the United States entered World War Two, it continued to increase its airborne forces even more as the four parachute battalions were expanded to regiments and the new 505th, 506th, 507th, 508th and 511th Parachute Regiments were formed, while, in August 1942, the 82nd and 101st Airborne Divisions were formed. In addition to parachute regiments, glider infantry regiments, airborne artillery and airborne engineers, other specialist troops were also assigned to the new airborne divisions. Even parachute-qualified MPs proved necessary since the paratroopers did not take well to discipline from 'leg' MPs.

During 1943, the 513th, 515th and 517th Parachute Regiments and the 11th, 13th and 17th Airborne Divisions were formed. By 1943, the 88th, 187th, 188th, 193rd, 194th, 325th, 326th, 327th and 401st Glider Infantry Regiments had also been formed.

The baptism of fire for American paratroopers had come in November 1942, when men of the 509th Parachute Infantry Battalion (PIB) jumped over North Africa. On 10 May 1943, the 82nd Airborne Division arrived in North Africa where they trained for future combat jumps. Two regiments from the 82nd soon got their chance to put this training into practice when the 504th PIR (Parachute Infantry Regiment) and 505th PIR jumped on 9 and 10 July 1943 during the invasion of Sicily.

Later, in September 1943, men of the 82nd's 504th, 505th and 509th PIR made another combat jump over Italy. By spring 1944, members of the 82nd Airborne Division had joined their comrades of the 101st Airborne Division in Britain to prepare for the invasion of Normandy. On 6 June 1944, men of both divisions jumped to capture key bridges, knock out German gun emplacements and carry out other important missions ahead of the invasion forces coming in over the beaches. A little over two months later, American paratroops of the 509th PIB, 517th PIR and 551st PIB jumped into combat again as they spearheaded the invasion of the South of France.

As soon as they were brought back up to strength after the Normandy drop, the paratroopers of the 82nd and 101st Airborne Divisions began preparing for another drop. This time the target was a group of key bridges in Holland. During Operation MARKET GARDEN both the 82nd and 101st made combat jumps along with the British 1st Airborne Division, which would be decimated at Arnhem.

Once again the 82nd and 101st Airborne Divisions were pulled back from the front lines. Both divisions were committed, however, to blunt the German onslaught during the Ardennes Offensive. In fact, the defense of Bastogne by the 101st became one of the legendary feats of US arms.

The final major American jump in the European Theater involved the 17th Airborne Division which had arrived in the UK in September 1944. On 24 March 1945, members of the 17th Airborne jumped near Wesel, Germany, during Operation VARSITY which struck across the Rhine.

While the 17th, 82nd and 101st Airborne Divisions had been seeing combat in Europe, the 13th Airborne Division, including the black 555th Parachute Infantry, had been training in the USA and the 11th Airborne Division had been seeing action in the Pacific. In September 1943, the 503rd PIR of the 11th made the first major American jump of the Pacific Campaign on New Guinea. The 503rd followed up with another jump on 3 and 4 July 1944, over Noemfoor Island. The final major American jumps in the Pacific took place in February 1945, when the 511th PIR jumped over Luzon and the 503rd PIR jumped to recapture Corregidor in a classic airborne assault upon a fortified island.

After the end of hostilities, the 11th Airborne Division was the first unit to enter Japan for occupation duties. The 13th Airborne had sailed to France in January 1945, but did not make a combat jump before the German surrender. As part of the XVIII Airborne Corps, the 82nd and 101st Airborne Divisions along with the 17th Airborne Division, which had arrived in Germany via parachute during Operation VARSITY, saw action in 1945 during the conquest of Germany but made no further combat jumps. The 13th was redeployed to the USA for use in the Pacific, but the Japanese surrender made their use unnecessary.

Soon after the end of hostilities, the 13th, 17th and 101st Airborne Divisions were quickly deactivated. The 82nd returned to the USA in January 1946, while the 11th Airborne Division remained in Japan until 1949.

The next action for American paratroopers was during the Korean War when the 187th Airborne Regimental Combat Team made combat jumps in October 1950 and March 1951. The 'Rakkasans' had served during the occupation as part of the 11th Airborne Division in Japan and, hence, were no strangers to the Far East.

After the Korean War, the 11th Airborne Division was deployed to Germany in 1956 but was deactivated in 1958. To keep an airborne capability in Europe, however, the 2nd Airborne Brigade/24th Infantry Division was formed from elements of the 11th Airborne Division. In July 1958, this brigade was deployed to Lebanon as part of American forces sent there.

In 1956, the 101st Airborne Division had also been reactivated. To replace the 2nd Airborne Brigade/24th Infantry Division, the 1st Airborne Brigade/8th Infantry Division was activated as the US airborne force assigned to NATO. Composed of the 1/509 AIR (Airborne Infantry Regiment), 2/509 AIR and 3/509 AIR, the 1st Airborne Brigade was stationed at Mainz until 1973. After August 1973, only the 3/509 (redesignated as the 1/509) remained an airborne unit. Stationed in Vicenza, Italy, this unit was later designated the Airborne Battalion Combat Team with its airborne infantry battalion redesignated the 4/325 and with airborne artillery and other support elements attached.

In April 1965, the 82nd Airborne Division was called upon to act as trouble shooters in the Dominican Republic where elements of the division remained until September 1966.

May 1965 saw the 173rd Airborne Brigade deployed to Vietnam where the unit remained until August 1971. Although the 173rd served primarily in the airmobile role in Vietnam, this unit made the only major parachute jump of the war in February 1967, as part of Operation JUNCTION CITY. The 3rd Brigade of the 82nd Airborne Division and the 101st Airborne Division also served in Vietnam. The 1st Brigade of the 1st Cavalry Division (Airmobile) was also an airborne unit when the 1st Cav was deployed to Vietnam. Though fully parachute qualified, airborne troops in Vietnam normally served in either the airmobile role or as elite light infantry. In August 1968, the 101st Airborne Division was redesignated as an airmobile rather than an airborne division and retains this designation today, though a proportion of the 101st remains parachute qualified.

After the Vietnam War, the 82nd Airborne Division and the Airborne Battalion Combat Team remained the only two US airborne units, though, of course, other parachute qualified units such as the Rangers and Special Forces existed to perform special missions.

The 82nd Airborne Division has seen its importance in American military planning continue to grow. As the US Army's most readily deployable division, the 82nd plays an important role in the Rapid Deployment Force and was used most recently during Operation URGENT FURY when paratroopers of the 82nd fought in Grenada.

The US airborne troops have almost half a century of tradition to live up to and when their wings are pinned on after completing three weeks of parachute training at Fort Benning, they wear them with immense pride. Two phrases which are drilled into any US paratrooper sum up the aggressive spirit which has made the US paratrooper such a formidable fighting man — 'All the way!' and 'Drive on, Airborne!'

1

BLANDFORD WAR PHOTO-FILES

FORMATION

1. During April 1941, men of the 501st Parachute Battalion, which had evolved from the original Parachute Test Platoon, check their T-4 model chutes prior to a jump at Ft Benning, Georgia. Note the soft aviator-style helmets and goggles and the one-piece jump smock.

2. Prior to a jump at Ft Benning in 1941, members of the 501st Parachute Battalion check their equipment, in this case the reserve chute of one of the jumpers.

3. Capt. J.W. Counts, who as a colonel later commanded the 513th Parachute Infantry Regiment, checks the chutes of members of the 501st Parachute Battalion prior to a jump in April 1941. Note the parachutist's insignia worn on the left side of his garrison cap.

1

2

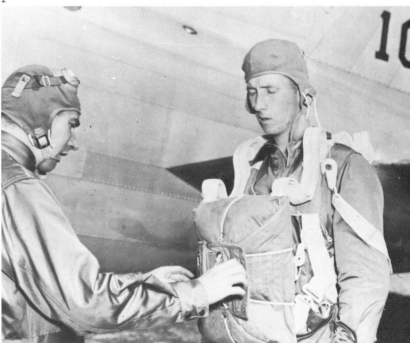

3

4. Members of the 501st Parachute Battalion board a C-47 at Lawson Field prior to a jump in April 1941.

5. Members of the 501st Parachute Battalion demonstrate landing techniques at Ft Benning during April 1941. Note how lightly equipped the man at right leaving the drop zone is.

4

5

6. Member of the 501st Parachute Battalion collapses his chute after landing at Ft Benning in April 1941.

7. Members of the 501st Parachute Battalion retrieve their equipment from an equipment roll after jumping at Ft Benning in April 1941. Note that, like German and Japanese paratroopers, the American paratroopers jump with a pistol, in this case a 1911A1 .45 auto.

8. Insignia of Airborne Command which was formed in March 1942 at Ft Benning under Col. Lee and which was in charge of all US airborne troops.

6

9, 10. Basic US parachutist's wings designed in 1941 by William Yarborough and still worn today, and, *right*, pathfinder wings.

11. US paratrooper in full jump gear, including the 'suit, two-piece, man's, parachutist' and highly polished jump boots. The weapon is the M1 Carbine

8

9

10

11

12. Member of the 501st Parachute Battalion descending from the 250-foot training tower at Ft Benning. Note that the original members of the Parachute Test Platoon had practiced on a 125-foot tower located at the Safe Parachute Company facility in Hightstown, New Jersey.

13. In June 1941, a trainee parachutist is strapped into his harness and waiting for his chute to be raised to the top of the 250-foot training tower and released.

14. Early airborne troops from Ft Benning practice glider tactics at the Air Force's experimental center at Wright Field.

12

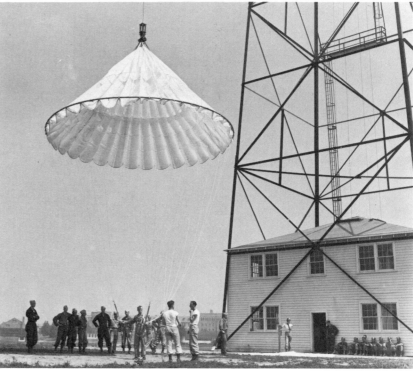

13

14

2

BLANDFORD WAR PHOTO-FILES

THE MEDITERRANEAN

15. 26 July 1943: Maj. Gen. Matthew Ridgeway, CO of the 82nd Airborne Division, along with two of his aides in Sicily. Curiously, Ridgeway appears to be wearing a shoulder sleeve insignia for the 9th Armored Division, which did not even arrive in the European Theater until August 1944. The aides both wear 82nd Airborne insignia. General Ridgeway has followed the general officers' prerogative and is wearing a revolver in his shoulder holster rather than an issue .45 auto.

16. On 25 July 1943 Maj. Gen. Ridgeway and members of his staff discuss the situation on a hill overlooking the battlefield near Riberia, Sicily. Note that here the general wears 82nd Airborne SSI. Note also the camouflaged helmets and the M1A1 'paratrooper's' Carbine in the jeep's scabbard.

15

16

17. Members of the 82nd Airborne Division pack and inspect cargo chutes in Morocco before a practice jump in June 1943.

18. Members of the 82nd Airborne Division board a C-47 prior to a practice jump in French Morocco during June 1943. Although the M1A1 Carbine and Thompson SMG were both widely used by US paratroopers, note that these men carry the M1 Garand.

17

18

19. Members of the 82nd Airborne Division loading chute-pack equipment on the belly of a C-47 transport aircraft prior to a practice jump in French Morocco during June 1943.

20. Members of the 505th Parachute Infantry, 82nd Airborne Division, emplaning onto a C-47 prior to a jump in French Morocco during June 1943.

21. 82nd Airborne paratroopers make a mass parachute drop at Oujda Airport, French Morocco, during June 1943.

20

21

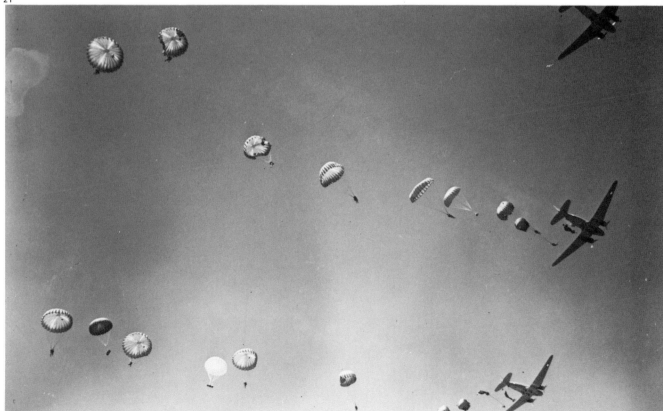

22. 82nd Airborne 'glider riders' lift the tail of a Waco glider prior to loading equipment into the nose during invasion training in French Morocco during June 1943.

23. Members of the 82nd Airborne Division prepare to load a 75mm pack howitzer aboard a Waco glider through the nose during pre-invasion training in French Morocco during June 1943.

24. Members of Battery A, 320th Glider Artillery Battalion, 82nd Airborne Division, seated in a glider after loading in their 75mm howitzer in June 1943 in French Morocco.

25. Gliders over Oujda Airport during pre-invasion training in French Morocco by the 82nd Airborne Division during June 1943.

24

25

26. Two paratroopers of a mass jump by troops of the 82nd Airborne Division during training in French Morocco during June 1943.

27. Member of the 82nd Airborne Division demonstrating proper landing technique during training in French Morocco in June 1943.

28. During the invasion of Sicily members of the 82nd Airborne move into the town of Sciacca.

29. Members of Battery A, 320th Glider Field Artillery, 82nd Airborne Division, back a jeep into the nose of a glider during training in French Morocco during June 1943.

26

27

28

30. 82nd Airborne paratroopers advancing on the town of Sciacca during the invasion of Sicily. A common practice among airborne troops was to commandeer transportation, and it appears that this is what these 'All Americans' have done.

31. Hat patches worn on the side of the garrison cap by American glider troops, left; parachute troops, middle; and parachute/glider troops with dual qualification, right. Parachute infantry wore a blue background, while artillery wore red.

30

31

3

BLANDFORD WAR
PHOTO-FILES

THE INVASION
OF EUROPE

32. Brig. Gen. Maxwell Taylor accompanies Winston Churchill on an inspection of the 101st Airborne Division at Newbury, Berkshire, UK, during March 1944. The 101st was in training at the time for the Normandy invasion.

33. Members of a glider unit of the 101st Airborne Division ready for take off during maneuvers at Greenham Common, UK, in October 1943.

34. US paratrooper who has just landed in Normandy on 6 June 1944.

35. Members of the 101st Airborne Division prior to emplaning for the drop over Normandy as part of the D-Day invasion. The censor has deleted their shoulder insignia.

33

34

35

36. US paratroopers going out of the door in a practice jump shortly before the Normandy invasion.

37. Member of the 82nd Airborne Division passes a French woman as he moves inland to engage the Germans after landing on occupied soil during the Normandy invasion. Note that his weapon is the Thompson SMG.

38. 82nd Airborne Division casualties being evacuated at Utah Beach during the invasion of Normandy. Note the German PoWs in the background.

37

39. After landing near Cherbourg on D-Day, these three American paratroopers dodged German patrols for 17 days. The men, who had been scavenging for food, enjoy their first regular meal in over two weeks.

40. Waco glider in flight during August 1944. Almost 14,000 CG-4A gliders were produced and though not a particularly attractive craft to look at, it proved quite functional. Among its other advantages were that pilots could be trained to fly it quickly and it could be loaded and unloaded quickly.

41. Member of the 101st Airborne Division along with a French officer during the liberation of France.

39

40

42. Officers of the 82nd Airborne Division receive a briefing before taking off for Operation MARKET GARDEN, the airborne invasion of Holland.

43. Maj. Gen. Maxwell Taylor, the CO of the 101st Airborne Division, has his parachute harness adjusted prior to emplaning for a drop over Eindhoven as part of Operation MARKET GARDEN. Note the 101st Airborne SSI on the man at the right along with the parachutist's hat patch. The man on the left wears the belt scabbard used by paratroopers to carry the folding stock M1A1 Carbine.

42

43

44. On 17 September 1944, Brig. Gen. James Gavin, the CO of the 82nd Airborne Division, checks his harness before emplaning for the drop over Nijmegen as part of Operation MARKET GARDEN. Note that Gavin chose to carry a full-sized M1 Garand rather than an M1 Carbine or a Thompson SMG.

45. Members of the 101st Airborne Division's pathfinder unit have been dropped by parachute near Bastogne and are now setting up radio equipment for guiding in aircraft with medical supplies and ammunition which will be dropped to the besieged division. This photograph was taken on 23 December 1944.

46. During the Battle of the Bulge members of the 101st Airborne Division march towards Haufflige, Belgium, where they will be committed to stem the German onslaught. Note the number of Bazookas visible since the paratroopers expect to find themselves facing German panzers.

44

45

46

47. On Christmas Eve 1944, members of the 101st Airborne Division sing carols despite enemy shelling of Bastogne where they are besieged.

48. On Christmas Day 1944, members of the 101st Airborne Division staff have Christmas dinner despite the German siege of Bastogne where they are located. Brig. Gen. Anthony McAuliffe (fourth from the left) was in command of the division in the absence of Gen. Taylor and will always be remembered for telling the German officer asking for his surrender, 'Nuts!'

49. On Christmas Day 1944, members of the 101st Airborne Division move through the ruins of buildings in Bastogne bombed on Christmas Eve. Dead members of the division lie along the road.

50. Members of the 101st Airborne Division move out of Bastogne to launch a counter-attack against the besieging Germans.

49

50

51

52

51. Following a night skirmish near Bastogne on 31 December 1944, members of the 101st Airborne Division set out to rejoin their unit.

52. On 31 December 1944, members of the 101st Airborne Division move out of Bastogne where they have been besieged for the last ten days to counter-attack against the Germans.

53. General officers of the 101st Airborne Division greet each other on 5 January 1945 after the German siege of Bastogne had been broken.

54. A corporal of the 463rd Parachute Artillery Battalion, 327th Glider Infantry, takes time out on 11 January 1945 to wash his feet near Bastogne, Belgium, where he was involved in the defense of that key blocking point.

55. Members of the 504th PIR, 82nd Airborne Division, move up on Herresbach by way of a firebreak in the woods on 28 January 1945.

53

54

55

56. A member of the 17th Airborne Division, then assigned to the US Third Army, examines a German machine gun left behind in the town of Marnach, Luxembourg, which has just been taken on 31 January 1945.

57. On 29 January 1945 members of the 505th PIR, 82nd Airborne Division, take a break near Weneck, Belgium, to read *Stars And Stripes*.

58. Two members of the 17th Airborne Division repair their radio in a tent north of Wiltz, Luxembourg, on 2 February 1945.

56

57

58

4

BLANDFORD WAR
PHOTO-FILES

THE PACIFIC

59. Shoulder sleeve insignia of the 11th Airborne Division which spent the war in the Pacific Theater.

60. Members of the 11th Airborne Division prepare for the jump over Luzon on 3 February 1945. Note the folding stock M1 Carbine in the right foreground.

61. Paratroopers of the 11th Airborne Division jump over Luzon, Philippine Islands, on 3 February 1945. Paratroopers taking part in this operation were primarily from the 511th PIR.

59

60

61

62. Equipment carried by a mortar assistant gunner when jumping; this equipment was laid out for display by a member of the 503rd PIR of the 11th Airborne Division. In addition to the mortar bipod, one can see an M1 Garand rifle, a .45 acp pistol, four grenades, rations, rope, 200 rounds of ammunition and four edged weapons — a bayonet, machete, trench knife and parachutist's switch blade knife.

63. Two 75mm howitzer gun crews pinned down by Japanese fire while assembling their guns after the jump on Corregidor on 16 February 1945. These gunners are from the 462nd Airborne Artillery.

62

63

64. Paratroopers of the 503rd Parachute Infantry Regimental Combat Team landing on Corregidor on 16 February 1945.

65. Transports of the 54th Troop Carrier Wing release men of the 3rd Battalion, 503rd Parachute Infantry Regiment, during the jump over Corregidor.

66. Members of the 503rd PIR moving over difficult terrain on Corregidor after their airborne assault on that island.

67. Two members of the 503rd PIR wait to see if the gasoline burning in the background will force any Japanese out of underground bunkers.

68. On 2 March 1945 Gen. Douglas MacArthur watches as members of the 503rd PIR raise the Stars and Stripes over Corregidor which they recaptured in an airborne assault.

69. A paratrooper of the 187th PIR, 11th Airborne Division, rests beside a dud parachute bomb during a lull in the fighting on Luzon in April 1945.

70. In May 1945 members of the 11th Airborne Division practice the proper method for exiting an aircraft door using a mockup.

69

71. 11th Airborne replacements at Lipa Airstrip, Batangas Province, Luzon, receive harness training during a one-week ground school set up by the division.

70

71

72

73

74

72. In June 1945, members of the 11th Airborne Division pass in review to honor Gen. Joseph Stilwell.

73. On 9 June 1945, members of the 11th Airborne Division make a mass jump in honor of Gen. Joseph Stilwell.

74. On 23 June 1945, men of the 511th PIR assemble after an airborne landing near Appari, in the Cagayan Valley on Luzon.

75. Members of the 511th PIR jumping from C-47s at Appari, Cagayan Valley, on Luzon on 23 June 1945. C-47s were the workhorses of the US paratroop forces in the Pacific as in Europe.

76. Members of the 511th PIR join forces with M-4 Sherman tanks of the 775th Tank Battalion after jumping into the Cagayan Valley on Luzon.

75

76

77. Members of the 11th Airborne Division jumping from a C-46 Commando over Luzon in July 1945 during a parachute and glider demonstration.

5

ACROSS
THE RHINE

78. Shoulder sleeve insignia of the 1st Allied Airborne which had been activated on 2 August 1944 by Gen. Eisenhower to have operational control over the IX Troop Carrier Command, the U.S. XVIII Airborne Corps consisting of the 17th, 82nd and 101st Airborne Divisions, all British airborne troops and British troop carrier formations. LTG Lewis Brereton commanded the 1st Allied Airborne Army.

79. Shoulder sleeve insignia of the 17th Airborne Division, the 'Talon from Heaven.'

80. US paratroopers prepare for a jump, probably across the Rhine; note the life vest around the necks and the M1A1 Carbine in the hip scabbard.

81. On 21 March 1945 a jeep is backed into a glider in preparation for Operation VARSITY, the airborne strike across the Rhine into Germany. This glider belongs to one of the units of the 17th Airborne Division.

78

79

80

81

83. Members of the 17th Airborne Division, rifle and Bazooka in hands, warm up after the jump across the Rhine.

84. 17th Airborne Division glider mechanic replaces the windshield of a glider in France during March 1945.

85. Members of the 17th Airborne Division lash smoke and incendiary grenades to the structural members of the interior of a glider prior to Operation VARSITY. These grenades can be discharged to camouflage the glider with smoke or, if necessary, to destroy it.

83

84

85

86. On 22 March 1945 members of the 17th Airborne Division lash down mortar rounds in a glider prior to the jump across the Rhine.

87. On 23 March 1945, Lieutenant Commander Stanley Johnson, Commanding Officer of the 139th Abn Engineer Battalion, 17th Airborne Division, briefs his men prior to the jump across the Rhine. The Marshalling Plan laid out at the left is of interest in showing the order, left then right, in which glider tugs took-off.

88. Paratroopers of the 17th Airborne Division prior to the jump across the Rhine; included are the visiting brass in the persons of (standing center left) Brig. Gen. J.T. Dalbey, 1st Allied Airborne Army; (standing center right) Brig. Gen. Ridgely Gaither, C.O. of the Parachute School at Ft Benning.

86

87

88

89. Members of the 17th Airborne Division move past abandoned German cars in the forest near Wesel on 24 March 1945 after their jump into Germany as part of Operation VARSITY.

90. View from a Waco glider of the 507th PIR, 17th Airborne Division, during the airborne invasion of Germany across the Rhine in Operation VARSITY on 24 March 1945.

91. German prisoners taken by men of the 513th PIR are lined up while a 17th Airborne paratrooper is in the foreground during Operation VARSITY.

92. Members of 'Raff's Ruffians', otherwise known as the 507th PIR, ride in a commandeered horse-drawn wagon during Operation VARSITY.

93. Members of the 17th Airborne Division assemble near Wesel on 24 March 1945 during Operation VARSITY.

91

92

93

106. At Mourmelon, France, members of the 466th Field Artillery, 17th Airborne Division, check each other's equipment before emplaning to jump during Operation VARSITY on 24 March 1945. Note that the officer at the right carries his .45 auto in a shoulder holster.

107. 75mm pack howitzer of the 466th Parachute Field Artillery packed under a C-47 ready for dropping during Operation VARSITY on 24 March 1945.

108. Members of the signal battalion attached to the 17th Airborne Division take cover from a German 88 during the airborne leap across the Rhine.

107

108

109

110

109. Paratroopers of the 194th Glider Infantry, 17th Airborne, move on after dealing with a German sniper hiding in a hayloft near Schermbeck, Germany, on 28 March 1945.

110. Paratroopers of the 17th Airborne Division along with Churchill tanks of the 6th Coldstream Guards advance into Muenster on 2 April 1945.

111. 17th Airborne troopers and British tankers keep careful watch as Germans who are surrendering run past in Muenster. The tank is a Churchill.

112. Members of the 17th Airborne Division pick up extra bandoliers of clips for their M1 rifles from behind a British Churchill just prior to entering Muenster on 2 April 1945.

111

112

113. Members of the 513th PIR, 17th Airborne Division, pass through a roadblock on the outskirts of Muenster on 2 April 1945. The next to last paratrooper carries a Browning machine gun.

114. Members of the 513th PIR await orders to advance into Muenster while Churchill tanks of the Coldstream Guards roll towards the city. Note that the paratrooper in the left foreground carries an M1A1 Carbine with stock opened and has an M3 Trench knife strapped to his right calf.

113

114

VICTORY
IN EUROPE

6

115. Members of the 82nd Airborne Division cross the Elbe at Bleckede, Germany, in Buffalo LVTs on 30 April 1945 on the way towards Berlin.

116. Maj. Gen. Maxwell Taylor, CO of the 101st Airborne Division, and Maj. Gen. Simon of the 13th SS Corps, complete the surrender of the remaining SS troops in the Schwendt area of Austria.

117. Maj. Gen. Chapman congratulates a member of the 326th Glider Infantry upon receipt of the Soldier's Medal. Note that the 13th Abn SSI is readily visible.

115

116

118. Maj. Gen. Chapman, CO of the 13th Airborne Division, presents the Soldier's Medal to a member of the 515th PIR in November 1944.

119. Maj. Gen. Chapman presenting the regimental colors of the 515th PIR to the regiment's commander Col. Julian Lindsey.

120. At Camp Mackall, North Carolina (named in honor of an American paratrooper killed in North Africa), Maj. Gen. E.G. Chapman (second from right) and his staff watch a review by members of the 13th Airborne Division, which Chapman commanded.

121. Members of the black 555th PIR being reviewed by Lieut. Gen. Ben Lear; Capt. James Porter of the 'triple nickel' is in the foreground and another member of the unit is visible in the background. The 555th was used as 'smoke jumpers' at one point to fight fires in the Northwestern US set by Japanese balloon bombs.

118

119

120

122. Members of the 82nd Airborne Division on a practice glider flight over France in March 1945.

123. US paratroopers preparing equipment for a drop, giving a good view of some airborne equipment, including the M1A1 Carbine worn in the belt scabbard.

122

123

124. US paratroopers making a practice jump from a C-46.

125. Officer of the 502nd Airborne Infantry Regiment accompanying a captured German. Note the 502nd pocket patch worn on the leather jacket and the parachute patch on the side cap.

126. Member of the 101st Airborne Division sets up a radio to direct C-47s which are about to drop supplies to the 4th Infantry Division in Germany during February 1945. Because of his assignment to work with the transport aircraft, it is possible this paratrooper was trained as a pathfinder.

127. Art experts assigned to the 101st Airborne Division examine paintings captured from the Germans.

124

125

126

127

128. On 2 April 1945, paratrooper Technical Sergeant Eric Swarzkoff questions a captured German officer taken in Appelhusen. Swarzkoff was possibly a field interrogator for the Counterintelligence Corps or perhaps just a German-speaking member of the unit. The fact Swarzkoff wears rank insignia would probably indicate he was not with CIC since its members normally did not wear rank insignia. Note the captured German pistol worn on his waist. The holster is of the type normally used for the Walther PP or PPK.

129. A company of the 101st Airborne Division passed in review at Mourmelon, France, on 15 March 1945 as the Division is awarded the Presidential Unit Citation.

130. Gen. Dwight D. Eisenhower and Maj. Gen. Maxwell Taylor, unit CO, review troops of the 101st Airborne Division in France on 15 March 1945.

129

130

131. U.S. paratroops stand in formation next to the 'Victory Bridge', completed by US combat engineers in six days to take the place of the wrecked Duisburg Bridge at the right in May 1945.

132. Members of the 101st Airborne Division at the Hotel Schiffmeister at Konigsee, Germany, try hard not to fraternize with the chambermaids in June 1945.

133. Maj. Gen. James Gavin, C.O. of the 82nd Airborne Division, reviews his troops near Reims, France, on 9 June 1945.

132

133

134. Maj. Gen. Maxwell Taylor, CO of the 101st Airborne Division, pins a star on the newly promoted Brig. Gen. William Gillmore, the division's artillery officer.

7

BLANDFORD WAR
PHOTO-FILES

OCCUPATION OF JAPAN

135

136

137

135. Five American servicemen captured by the Japanese at Corregidor welcome 11th Airborne troops at Atsugi Airstrip outside of Tokyo on 8 August 1945.

136. Three members of the 11th Airborne Division guard a canal in Yokohama, Japan, during September 1945. The 11th Airborne was the first US unit to occupy Japan.

137. Maj. Lewis Treadwell, CO of the 3rd Battalion, 188th PIR, 11th Airborne Division, reviews his battalion as it parades on a street in Yokohama on 8 September 1945.

138. A paratrooper of the 11th Airborne Division inspects captured Japanese ordnance at Sendai on 27 September 1945.

139. 11th Airborne Division signalman inspects captured Japanese signal equipment at Sendai on 27 September 1945.

138

139

140. Members of the 188th PIR, 11th Airborne Division, arrive in a C-54 on Atsugi on 30 August 1945.

141. 11th Airborne troops who have arrived on Atsugi via the C-54s visible at the right load onto trucks for transport to their billets.

142. Two paratroopers of the 188th PIR of the 11th Airborne stand guard at an intersection in Yokohama on 21 September 1945.

140

141

143

144   145

143. Members of the 511th PIR of the 11th Airborne break formation on Okinawa on 24 August 1945 before heading for occupation duties in Tokyo.

144. Members of the 511th PIR fall in for inspection on 24 August 1945 in preparation for moving into Tokyo.

145. Members of the 188th PIR loading their gear onto an AC-54 at Kadena airport prior to leaving for Tokyo on 29 August 1945.

146. Members of the 188th PIR, the lead man carrying a Browning MG, board an AC-54 for transport to occupation duties in Tokyo.

147

148

149

147. Members of the 188th PIR emplaning for transport to Tokyo. They wear lifevests since they will be passing over water.

148. Paratroopers of the 188th PIR, 11th Airborne Division, board an AC-54 transport on 29 August 1945 for transport to occupation duties in Japan.

149. Members of the 188th PIR hold retreat on the streets of Yokohama after arriving in Japan.

150. Secretary of War Robert P. Patterson watches a practice jump from a training tower during an inspection of the jump school of the 11th Airborne Division at Sendai, Japan, during January 1946.

151. 11th Airborne Division guard at Grant Hotel, General HQ in Yokohama, on 1 September 1945.

152. On 12 January 1946, the 82nd Airborne Division parades in triumph down New York City's Fifth Avenue.

151

152

8

BLANDFORD WAR
PHOTO-FILES

KOREA

153. Brig. General Charles Canham speaks before members of the 82nd Airborne Division at Fort Bragg, NC, on 28 November 1949. The 11th, in Japan until 1949, and the 82nd, in the USA, were the only Airborne Divisions retained after 1945.

154. Members of the 187th Airborne Regimental Combat Team prepare for a jump in Korea on 7 March 1951. Their uniforms and equipment differ little from those of their World War Two counterparts.

155. Members of the 187th Airborne Regimental Combat Team prepare for a jump in Korea. M1 Garand rifles are still used and the rucksack is slung beneath the reserve chute.

153

154

156. On 7 March 1951, members of the 2nd Battalion, 187th Airborne Regimental Combat Team, check equipment before boarding C-119s for a jump in Korea.

157. Members of the 187th Airborne Regimental Combat Team wait for take-off aboard a C-119 prior to a practice jump in Korea during March 1951.

156

157

BLANDFORD WAR
PHOTO-FILES

THE VIETNAM ERA

158. Distinctive insignia of 82nd Airborne Division (left) and 101st Airborne Division (right).

159. Airborne insignia locally-made in Vietnam for the 173rd Airborne Brigade (upper left), MACV Airborne advisors (upper right) and 101st Airborne (bottom).

160. Insignia made locally in Vietnam for snipers assigned to the three major airborne units serving in country: 82nd Airborne Division (top), 101st Airborne Division (bottom left) and 173rd Airborne Brigade (bottom right). Only the 3rd Brigade of the 82nd Airborne Division served in Vietnam.

158

159

160

161. MC-1 Parachutist's Knife, which can be opened with one hand since it is a 'switchblade' type. The hooked blade is included for use where a point might do damage.

162. A member of the 1st Battalion, 508th Airborne Infantry Regiment, 82nd Airborne Division, uses a flamethrower to destroy a house which had contained a heavily fortified enemy position during an operation near Trung Lap, Republic of Vietnam, on 18 June 1969.

161

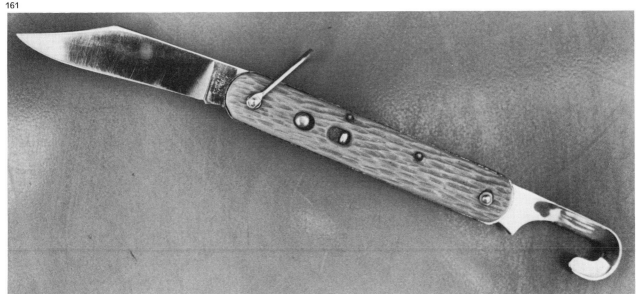

162

163. During Operation DIRTY DEVIL near Trung Lap in June 1969, members of the 508th Airborne Infantry of the 82nd Airborne Division scan a nearby woodline searching for enemy troops who have just fired upon a resupply helicopter. This operation probably takes its name from the red devil on the 508th's pocket patch.

164. During 1965, paratroopers of the 173rd Airborne Brigade hit an LZ (landing zone) during a search and destroy operation. The 173rd was the first major US Army combat unit committed to Vietnam.

165. In June 1969, members of the 321st Artillery, 82nd Airborne Division, pour fire onto enemy positions near Phu Bai, Republic of Vietnam. Note the flak jacket worn by the paratrooper at the left.

166. Paratroopers of the 173rd Airborne Brigade dash from their choppers during a search and destroy operation near Phuoc Tuy in 1965.

165

166

167. A grenadier of the 101st Airborne Division prepares to fire an M79 40mm grenade launcher during the Vietnam War.

168. Members of the 101st Airborne Division prepare to engage a target using a 3.5-inch rocket launcher, also known as the 'Super Bazooka.' This weapon was used in Vietnam primarily as a 'bunker buster' to destroy concrete or other heavy emplacements.

169. After dropping members of the 173rd Airborne Brigade for an operation south of Bien Hoa on 28 June 1965, choppers depart to pick up more troops.

167

168

170. During the assault on Hill 875 during November 1967, a dog handler of the 39th Scout Dog Platoon pauses with his dog to talk with members of the 4th Battalion of the 173rd Airborne Brigade who are carrying out the assault.

171. Members of the 503rd Airborne Infantry Regiment, 173rd Airborne Brigade, move into position at the base of Hill 881 near Dak To on 15 November 1967. The terrain they are moving through illustrates why ambush was a constant danger in many parts of Vietnam.

170

171

172. Shortly after arrival in the Republic of Vietnam, paratroopers of the 173rd Airborne Brigade move out of Bien Hoa Air Base to increase security in the area. This photograph, taken in May 1965, illustrates the newness of the 173rd to combat in Vietnam since they are too bunched together for proper anti-ambush drill and appear to be on a stroll rather than a patrol in a combat zone. The 173rd learned fast, though, since they saw a great deal of action during their years in Vietnam.

173. On 17 January 1967 during Operation CEDAR FALLS, members of the 503rd Airborne Infantry Regiment, 173rd Airborne Brigade, head for an area in the 'Iron Triangle' where an estimated platoon of Viet Cong are suspected of hiding in the Thanh Dien Forest. During February 1967, the 503rd made the only combat jump of the War by US paratroopers, except for insertions of recon teams and small clandestine jumps.

172

173

174. Near Dak To on 10 November 1967, members of the 1st Battalion, 503rd Airborne Infantry, dig in while under fire.

175. Members of the 173rd Airborne Brigade reach the top of a hill in the highlands of Dak To. The smoke at the left has been set off so that the spotter aircraft overhead know the location of the paratroopers.

176. Members of the 173rd Airborne Brigade destroy enemy bunkers after the assault on Hill 875 southwest of Dak To in November 1967.

177. Shortly after their arrival in Vietnam, mortarmen of the 2nd Battalion, 503rd Airborne Infantry, fire on Viet Cong positions north of Bien Hoa in May 1965.

178. Members of Troop E, 17th Cavalry, 173rd Airborne Brigade, fire their jeep-mounted 106mm recoilless rifle into a suspected enemy position during a road security mission in February 1969 near LZ 'English.'

176

177

178

179. Members of Troop E, 17th Cavalry, 173rd Airborne Brigade, fire a jeep-mounted M60 at an enemy position near LZ 'English', February 1969.

180. UH-1D Hueys bring in members of the 1st and 2nd Battalions, 503rd Airborne Infantry, of the 173rd Airborne Brigade during a search and destroy operation about 40 miles south of Saigon in August 1965. At this time, the 173rd had only been in Vietnam for a few months but was already seeing heavy use as an airmobile reaction force.

181. Members of the 173rd Airborne Brigade on their LZ south of Saigon during a search and destroy operation in August 1965. The trooper at the far right appears to be carrying a stretcher.

182. Members of the 503rd Airborne Infantry move out across rice paddies during a search and destroy mission after being airlifted into an area about 40 miles southeast of Saigon in August 1965. The terrain these paratroopers are moving through was typical of southeastern Vietnam.

181

182

183. Members of the 319th Artillery, 173rd Airborne Brigade, fire their 105mm howitzer at an area suspected to contain enemy troops during 1968.

184. In November 1967, members of the 173rd Airborne Brigade are pinned down by mortar fire during the assault on Hill 875, 15 miles southwest of Dak To (see **177**).

183

184

185. During the assault on Hill 875 a sergeant of the 173rd Airborne Brigade watches his unit's perimeter as he mans an M60 GPMG prior to the assault. The OD towel around his neck and bottle of 'bug juice' in the band around his helmet are both very typical of the 'grunt's' attempts to deal with the insects and heat so common in Vietnam.

186. Members of the 173rd Airborne Brigade move out after checking a hut in Binh Duong Province during a search and destroy operation late in September 1965.

10

BLANDFORD WAR PHOTO-FILES

RAPID DEPLOYMENT

187. Members of the 82nd Airborne Division prepare to attack the 'enemy' during Exercise SWIFT STRIKE III during August 1963. Members of the 82nd Airborne were armed with the M14 rifle at this time, and the muzzles of various M14s are visible.

188. During January 1963, communications specialists of the 503rd Airborne Infantry, 82nd Airborne Division, move up behind members of their unit during live fire exercises as part of SUNSHADE IV at Ft Bragg. Because of their rapid deployment mission, members of the 82nd Airborne traditionally train more realistically and more often than most other units.

189. Communications men check their contact during a lull in their company's attack during the 82nd Airborne's Exercise SUNSHADE IV in January 1963.

187

190. On 10 May 1965, the 82nd Airborne Division band marches through the 'Safety Corridor' (Line of Communication) in Santo Domingo, Dominican Republic. The 82nd Airborne had been sent in to help establish order in that country.

189

190

191. Shoulder sleeve insignia, XVIII Airborne Corps, stationed at Ft Bragg, North Carolina.

192. Coin carried by members of the XVIII Corps.

193. Coin carried by members of the 82nd Airborne Division and presented for inspection when requested by other unit members. Airborne coins are meant to build esprit de corps among current and former paratroopers and are surrounded with certain traditions. For example, failure to present one's coin may result in having to buy drinks for all other paratroopers present.

194. During a live fire exercise at Ft Bragg in July 1978, a member of the 4/68th Armor, 82nd Airborne Division, threads rounds into his Browning .50 caliber MG mounted atop his M551 Armored Recon Vehicle (Sheridan).

195. Members of the 82nd Airborne hit the chutes during a practice jump from a C-130 at Camp A.P. Hill.

191

192

193

194

196. During live fire exercises in July 1978, a member of the 82nd Airborne Division prepares to fire the Vulcan 20mm anti-aircraft system.

197. During 1979 members of the 82nd Airborne Division make a practice jump at Ft Bragg using the MC1-B-1 parachute.

198. A member of the 1st Battalion, 325th Airborne Infantry, fires an M72 LAW (Light Anti-Tank Weapon) during live fire exercises in October 1981.

199. Members of a combat support company of the 325th Airborne Infantry, 82nd Airborne, prepare a position for a 107mm mortar during live fire exercises in October 1981.

196

197

198

199

200. Members of the 1st Battalion, 325th Airborne Infantry, 82nd Airborne, prepare to move forward on the platoon assault course during live fire exercises in October 1981.

201. A member of the 1st Battalion, 325th Airborne Infantry Regiment, 82nd Airborne Division, moves forward during a live fire exercise on the platoon assault course during October 1981.

202. In June 1982, prior to the REFORGER exercise, members of the 3rd Brigade of the 82nd Airborne Division listen to a lecture by German officers. The man at the right wears a Jungle Expert pocket patch indicating completion of the jungle survival course in Panama.

203. In May 1983, a member of the 82nd Airborne Division learns the operation of the Soviet ZSU 23mm anti-aircraft gun during SOLID SHIELD OPERATIONS '83 at Camp Lejeune, North Carolina.

200

201

204. Members of the 82nd Airborne aboard a transport aircraft prior to a jump in Egypt during BRIGHT STAR exercises in 1981. The sand-colored helmet cover and desert pattern camouflage utilities are worn.

205. During BRIGHT STAR exercises in Egypt during 1981, a member of the 82nd Airborne Division checks another paratrooper's chute prior to a jump. The trooper at right wears the distinctive maroon beret of the 82nd Airborne. On his beret flash, he wears the distinctive insignia of his subunit. The shoulder sleeve insignia worn on his left sleeve is the subdued version of the 82nd Airborne insignia.

206. Member of the 82nd wearing the new 'Fritz' helmet emplaces an M18 Claymore mine.

207. Members of the 508th Airborne Infantry, 82nd Airborne Division, move through the woods during training at Ft Bragg, North Carolina. Note the use of local flora for camouflage to supplement the woodland BDUs (battle dress uniforms) worn by the 82nd.

208. While training during 1979 one member of the 82nd Airborne Division shows another

one the proper method for emplacing the M15 anti-tank mine.

209. During an exercise, a radioman of the 82nd Airborne Division checks his communications. He wears woodland camo pattern BDUs and the 'Fritz' ballistic helmet. His M16 has a blank firing device affixed at the muzzle.

210. With straw stuck in his helmet for additional camouflage, a member of the 82nd Airborne Division crouches behind cover during a training exercise at Ft Bragg recently.

207

208

209

211. During a recent training exercise, a grenadier of the 82nd Airborne Division armed with an M16 rifle with M203 40mm grenade launcher moves through the trees.

212. Members of the 82nd Airborne Division rapidly exit the rear of a C-130 aircraft during a jump.

213

214

213. During October 1975, as part of the BRAVE SHIELD XV exercises, a light tank is extracted from a C-130 using the LAPES (Low Altitude Parachute Extraction) technique, one method of dropping heavy equipment to airborne units.

214. Artillerymen of the 82nd Airborne Division fire on enemy positions during the invasion of Grenada in October 1983.

215. 82nd Airborne Division gunners firing on enemy positions with their M102, 105mm Light Howitzer during the October 1983 invasion of Grenada.

216. Paratroopers of the 82nd Airborne Division deploy on the Island of Grenada during the invasion of that country in October 1983. Although the 82nd did not make a combat jump on Grenada, members of the division did take part in the mopping up operations to secure the island. The grenadier at the rear wears the special vest for carrying 40mm grenades. All three troopers wear the 'Fritz' helmet which got its baptism of fire on Grenada and proved quite effective, saving the lives of at least a couple of paratroopers.

215

BIBLIOGRAPHY

Beckett, Brian. *The Illustrated History of the Vietnam War*, Blandford Press, Poole, 1985

Bowers, Michael (editor). *North American Fighting Uniforms*, Blandford Press, Poole, 1984.

Daniell, Rosemary, *Sleeping with Soldiers*, Granada, London, 1985.

Laughlin, Cameron and Langellier, John P. *US Army Uniforms: Europe 1944–45*, Uniforms Illustrated No.14, Arms and Armour Press, London.

Meisner, Arnold and Russell, Lee. *Modern American Soldier*, Uniforms Illustrated No.16. Arms and Armour Press, 1986.

Mollo, Andrew, and McGregor, Malcolm. *Army Uniforms of World War 2*. Blandford Press, Poole, 1981.

Smith, Digby and Chappell, Micheal. *Army Uniforms Since 1945*, Blandford Press, Poole, 1980.

Stanton, Shelby L. *Green Berets at War: US Army Special Forces in Asia 1956–1975*, Arms and Armour Press, London, 1986.

Thompson, Leroy and Chappell, Michael. *Uniforms of the Elite Forces*, Blandford Press, Poole, 1982.

Thompson, Leroy. *Elite Unit Insignia of the Vietnam War*. Arms and Armour Press, London, 1986.

Thompson, Leroy. *Uniforms of the Indo-China and Vietnam Wars*, Blandford Press, Poole, 1985.

Weeks, John. *The Airborne Soldier*, Blandford Press, Poole, 1982.

INDEX